46

SPEEDRUN MINECRAFT

Just how fast do you reckon you can go?!

78

BONUS SURVIVAL SEEDS

These might just come in handy!

WELCOME

Hello and welcome to our book, which is jam packed with as much Minecraft goodness as we could squeeze onto its pages!

We've got tonnes to talk about! We'll be pretty much going through everything to do with the world's best videogame, and giving you loads of tips to help you on your adventuring.

Whether you're just getting started with Minecraft or are a seasoned pro, you should find lots here to help you on your way, whichever mode of the game you love to play.

Of course, the best thing about Minecraft is just how much there is to do, so we wish you the very best with your exploring. Don't forget to stay safe out there, though - you never know when a dastardly creeper might be lurking around the corner!

Enjoy your Minecrafting. Now turn the page and let's get down to business!

HOW TO...
QUICKLY FIND
DIAMONDS

> Diamonds make the best gear, so how can you pick up these rare resources quickly?

EXPLORE LAVA LAKES

Lava lakes form at roughly the same level as diamond ore. So if you encounter some lava underground, mine around the edges and you're sure to find some diamonds due to the way the lake carves out huge chunks of the subterranean landscape. Just take care not to slip in while you're exploring, and don't let those precious diamonds drop into the lava when you break the ore!

TREASURE CHESTS

as long as it makes sense, then mine three blocks to your left and right, and come back on yourself. This allows you to see the most efficient number of blocks and maximise your chance of finding diamonds.

TREASURE CHESTS

Diamonds can appear in a huge number of treasure chests, but the easiest ones to get your hands on are found in desert temple chests and village weaponsmith/ toolsmith chests. If you're comfortable exploring shipwrecks, the treasure chests there are also likely to contain diamonds (plus other useful items like emeralds, iron ingots and gold ingots!). The good thing about these chests is that they're often easy to get even early on in the game, and quick to uncover, whereas mining for diamonds can take a long time and require a lot of work!

TIP: Armourer, toolsmith and weaponsmith villagers will trade one diamond for one emerald, depending on their skill level.

STRIP MINING

Digging for diamonds is slow but almost guaranteed to yield results, with the added bonus that you'll collect a lot of redstone and other ores while you're searching! To strip mine, head to the low levels of the map where diamond ore is more common, and dig long tunnels that are two blocks high by one block wide. Keep digging in a single direction for

STRIP MINING

CHEAT!

If all else fails, use the command console! Just type "/give @p minecraft:diamond 64" to get a full stack of diamonds added to your inventory. It might not be the most fun or rewarding way to get diamonds, but if you're desperate for them at short notice it's a foolproof way to fill your inventory!

CHEAT!

Though if cheats are enabled and used in your world, you may not get some achievements.

TIP: Having the Fortune enchantment on your pickaxe allows you to collect extra items when you break an ore block – and it works on diamonds!

HOW TO...
NEVER GET
LOST

Navigating around the world of Minecraft is always tough, so here are some ways you can stop yourself from getting lost!

COMPASSES

Crafted from four iron ingots and one redstone dust, the red part of a compass always points back to the world spawn point, which is the place you first appeared when you entered the newly generated world. Hopefully, knowing that will allow you to make your way back to familiar territory no matter where you find yourself! Compasses don't work in the Nether or the End – at least not at first…

LODESTONES

Surround a Netherite ingot with chiseled stone bricks to craft a lodestone block. Using a compass on the lodestone causes the compass to take on a blue glow and always point to the lodestone. This works in the Overworld, the Nether and the End, so as long as you have a compass and the lodestone remains intact, you can always find your way back to where you placed the lodestone!

TIP: Lodestones can be found in some of the loot chests in Bastion Remnants in the Nether.

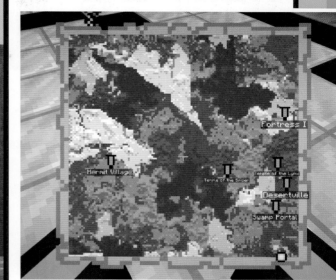

MAP MARKERS

In the Java Edition, "use" a map on a banner to place a marker on the map. The marker appears in the base colour of the banner. If you rename the banner on an anvil, the marker will also be named.
  Sadly, this doesn't work in the Bedrock Edition, however in both versions you can create a map marker by placing a framed copy of a map within the map's boundaries.

TIP: You can place a map in the offhand slot to get a minimap version as part of your interface.

MAPS

A map can easily be crafted from eight sheets of paper surrounding a compass. Looking at the map fills in the surrounding terrain. There are five zoom levels, which increase if you craft the map with an additional eight pieces of paper (or just one piece if you use a cartography table).
  At the closest zoom level, every block is represented by one pixel on the map. At zoom level 5, each pixel on the map represents 16 blocks. Maps of the same zoom level can be placed in frames that match up, to view even larger areas.

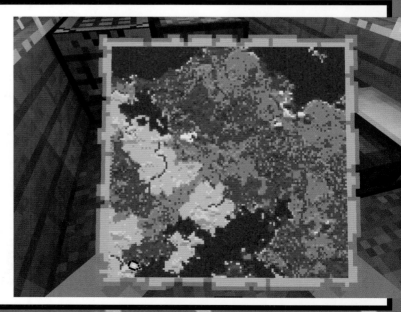

HOW TO...
FIND HIDDEN LOOT

There's secret treasure all over Minecraft, if you know where to look!

BURIED TREASURE MAPS

If you explore the chests found in underwater ruins or shipwrecks, you're bound to pick up a buried treasure map. This shows a location nearby where you can find a buried chest! The map starts out with an outline of the terrain, which fills in as you get closer. If you dig where the X is, you'll eventually find a chest filled with riches. It can take a lot of work to find the right spot – try to make sure the front of your map marker is just touching the centre of the X when you're digging!

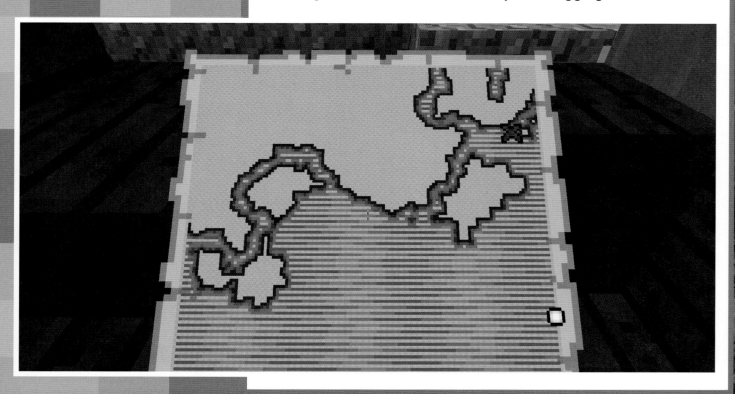

WOODLAND MANSION SECRETS

Some rooms in woodland mansions contain chests, but the real treasures are the hidden blocks! The secret obsidian room contains a small pile of obsidian with a diamond block in the centre. Likewise, the secret lava room has a pool of lava surrounded by glass, with a diamond block in the centre. In illager statue rooms, simply break the illager's wool head to find a lapis lazuli block!

TIP: Pay 14 emeralds and a compass to a Journeyman-level cartographer to get hold of a map to a woodland mansion.

JUNGLE TEMPLES

Jungle temples contain two chests: one protected by traps and the other hidden. Both are on the bottom floor of a temple, and finding the first involves cutting tripwires with shears to avoid activating traps. The second is uncovered using a lever system. When you come down the stairs, you'll see levers on your right or your left. Start by flicking the lever furthest from the staircase, then the one closest, then flick that one again before flicking the furthest again. Ignore the middle one and the chest will be uncovered.

TIP: Half of all igloos have a basement that contains treasure – check under the carpet!

DESERT TEMPLES

Finding the loot in desert temples is simple, but dangerous! Each temple has a pattern of stained terracotta on the floor, with a deep pit beneath it. Directly below the blue block is a pressure plate, which, if triggered, will set off nine blocks of TNT at the base of the pit, destroying the treasure (and probably you!). Be careful to dig your way down the edge of the pit, lighting the inside so no mobs can spawn and trigger the pressure plate, then you'll get to open no fewer than four treasure chests!

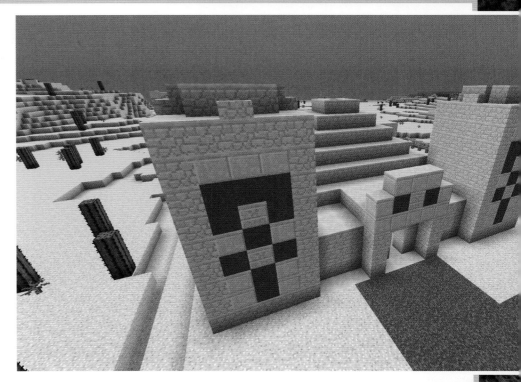

HOW TO...
LEVEL UP FAST

Collecting experience orbs unlocks the ability for advanced enchantments and repairs, so how can you level up quickly?

KILLING MOBS
Whether a mob is hostile, neutral or tame, you almost always get experience from killing them. The only exceptions are villagers, golems, bats and all baby mobs! You can collect the experience if you kill the mob or it's killed by a tame wolf. The default amount of experience per mob is 1-3 for friendly ones and 3-5 for hostile ones, though if a hostile mob has spawned with equipment (such as armour) it will drop +3 experience for each piece.

KILL A PLAYER

If you're playing a PvP game, killing another player will net you 7 experience points for every level they have, up to a maximum of 700 points. Remember the same applies to you, so stay out of the way of other players! If you die, you can collect this experience yourself, though. Just like you drop your items when you die, you also drop experience. Quickly return to where you fell, and you'll be able to collect 7 points per experience level, just like any other player would.

TIP: The first time you kill the ender dragon, you'll receive 12,000 experience points!

BREAK A MOB SPAWNER

You can collect experience by mining ore and other special blocks, but when you find a mob spawner you collect a bigger chunk of experience by getting close and smashing it —15-43 points as long as you use a pickaxe to break it! However, hanging around and killing mobs as they spawn will allow you to keep on collecting experience, so only smash spawners you're unlikely to revisit!

BOTTLES O' ENCHANTING

The rare bottle o' enchanting is a bottle of magical liquid, similar to a splash potion, although instead of adding an effect to its target, it drops 3-11 experience orbs when it breaks. You can only get the bottle by either trading three emeralds with a Master-level cleric, or finding it as treasure in pillager outposts and shipwrecks (in the Java Edition) or in buried treasure chests using a map (in the Bedrock Edition).

TIP: Ravagers drop the most experience of any non-boss mob – 20 points per kill.

HOW TO... RIDE HORSES

Riding horses is quick, efficient AND fun, but first they have to trust you...

TAMING HORSES

Horses, which spawn in the Plains and Savanna biomes, can be tamed quite easily. First, approach the horse with an empty hand. Now interact with it to climb on its back, at which point it will attempt to throw you off by rearing up. When this happens, simply get back on the horse and repeat the process until hearts rise from its head. When this happens, you've tamed the beast and are almost ready to ride it!

SADDLING HORSES

Once a horse has been tamed, you need to get a saddle onto its back. Saddles are collected from a number of places. You can get them from several sets of loot chests, as a treasure item while fishing, by trading with a leatherworker, or by killing a ravager. They can be used to ride horses, as well as donkeys, mules, pigs and striders.

To saddle a horse, tame it, then sit on its back and open up the inventory. Drag the saddle into the relevant armour slot, then you'll be able to control its direction!

TIP: Horses, donkeys and mules can all be tamed and ridden in exactly the same way!

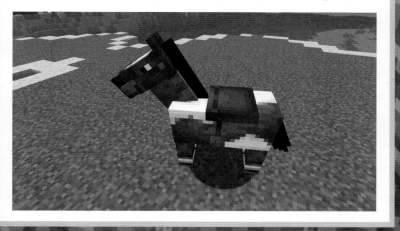

MULES

Although they don't spawn on their own, you can create a mule by breeding together a horse and a donkey. They're stronger and faster than donkeys and smaller than horses, and while they can't wear horse armour they CAN carry a chest. As in real life, mules can't breed with horses, donkeys or other mules. To equip a chest on a mule (or donkey), you have to use the chest on it, as it can't be equipped using the inventory like armour and a saddle!

TIP: Horses can be equipped with horse armour and saddles, while donkeys and mules can be equipped with a chest and saddle.

HORSE HEALTH

Horses, donkeys and mules have a health value of 15-30 points, and can be fed certain food items to restore health points. Sugar restores 1 point, wheat 2 points, apples 3 points, golden carrots 4 points, golden apples 10 points, and hay bales 20 points. Unlike the other foodstuffs, hay bales can't be fed to untamed horses, while golden carrots and golden apples also put horses into love mode, allowing them to breed.

21 BUILD TIPS

Learn to build like an expert with our best tips, tricks and shortcuts!

4
STAIRS MAKING A SLOPED ROOF

1 Always plan a build first, whether on paper, a wall plan on the ground, or just visualising it in your head!

2 For most builds, the ideal height of a room is three or four blocks.

3 Sticking to one or two materials makes your builds look cohesive and well designed.

4 Use stair blocks to make a sloped roof, and as a bonus you get an attic space inside!

5 Place double doors to make the main entrance obvious.

6 Flatten the land around your build, as it makes it easier to expand and decorate.

7 Be creative with light sources – don't just cover your walls in torches. Mix it up with lamps, lanterns, candles and more.

8 Use signs to create atmosphere and prompt expectations. Labelling a room can transform how you see it.

9 Don't use basic blocks like cobblestone and dirt to build. Remember that many blocks have a polished or decorative variant.

10 Automate doors with pressure plates to make navigating your base easy (although don't put one outside, otherwise it will let in unwanted mobs!).

11 Running four or five furnaces can help you smelt much more quickly, so don't stop once you've made your first.

12 If you want to make an area look overgrown, sprinkle bone meal on grass blocks to create long grass.

13 Trapdoors hold back water, so you can use them to create bathtubs or troughs.

10 PRESSURE PLATE DOOR

14 DAYLIGHT SENSOR LAMPPOST

14 Place a daylight sensor on top of a redstone lamp and it will automatically illuminate itself at night.

15 Banners hung at the sides of windows will look like curtains.

16 A piston, pointing upwards and powered from below, makes a decent table.

17 Mobs can jump over iron bars, but not fences or walls, so use the latter as a perimeter.

18 Place blank signs on the side of wood stairs to create small armchairs and sofas – the signs look like armrests.

19 Carpet tiles can be used to hide light sources – they cover the block but let the light through.

20 Flatten grass blocks with a shovel to create paths.

21 The patterns on glazed terracotta can be rotated and repurposed (magenta terracotta has arrows built into it), but they also form repeating tiled patterns.

21 GLAZED TERRACOTTA PATTERNS

HOW TO...
WORK WITH
REDSTONE

Redstone lets you make complicated circuits and machinery, so here's how to get to grips with the basics

REDSTONE POWER SOURCES

Redstone power is like electricity, so you need a power source to use it. Power sources can be solid blocks of redstone dust, which continually emit redstone power, but they can also be triggers such as buttons, which emit a short pulse of redstone when pressed, or levers, which turn redstone power on and off when flipped. Some objects emit redstone power as a side effect,

REDSTONE POWER SOURCES

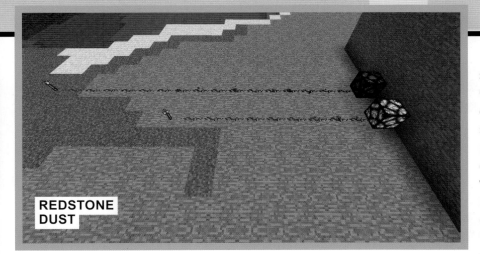

REDSTONE DUST

signal. Other components, such as TNT, pistons or dispensers, will activate when they receive a redstone signal. You can use redstone to turn on lamps, open and close doors, or activate and deactivate hoppers. A huge number of components can be used as redstone components – try experimenting with them to see what happens!

such as a trapped chest, which acts like a normal chest but emits a redstone pulse when opened. Perhaps the most useful power source is a redstone torch, which emits power when active, but can itself be turned on or off by receiving a redstone pulse.

REDSTONE DUST

If redstone power is like electricity, redstone dust is like the wires. You can lay trails of dust from any power source, and the power will travel along it. A full-strength signal will travel for 15 blocks, and the strength of the signal diminishes by one point for every block's distance it travels. Redstone dust can be mined directly from redstone ore, found deep underground.

TIP: Striking redstone ore causes it to light up briefly.

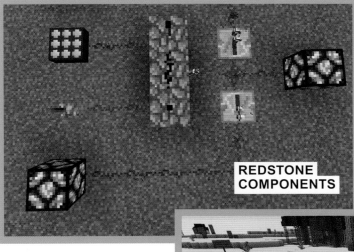

REDSTONE COMPONENTS

TARGETS

If you put four pieces of redstone dust around a hay bale, you create a target block. These are a type of redstone trigger that outputs a redstone signal when struck by an

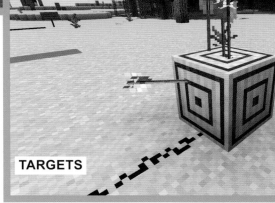

TARGETS

REDSTONE COMPONENTS

There are a lot of redstone components, some of which affect blocks and others which are part of circuitry. Redstone repeaters can boost a weak signal for a further 15 blocks, while redstone comparators can test which signal is stronger as part of a circuit, or turn a block's status (e.g. how full a chest is) into a redstone

arrow or some other projectile. The fun part is they output a redstone signal with a strength based on how close to the centre of the target the weapon hits!

TIP: Surround a glowstone block with four redstone dust to make a redstone lamp.

HOW TO...
CRAFT FURNITURE

BATHTUB

Place trapdoors – birch ones are usually the best choice – on the floor, then "open" them so they stand up and enclose a 3x2 space. You can then place water source blocks inside! If you're close to a wall, finish off your bathtub by using tripwire hooks as "taps".

GRANDFATHER CLOCK

Use wood blocks or logs to build a 3x1 post, then place item frames on the front of it. Put a clock in the top frame, a stick in the middle frame and an iron spade in the bottom frame. Rotate the stick and the spade so they're vertical, then they'll look like a pendulum!

CURTAINS

You can make curtains easily! Just place a banner either side of a window and watch them sway gently in the breeze. Of course, you won't be able to close them, but it's a small price to pay for such elegance!

TIP: Place two beds next to each other to make a double bed!

DESK LAMP

Place a fence post (or any similar item, such as a single iron bar or chain) on a desk, then put a sea lantern on top of it. Now attach trapdoors to every side of the sea lantern. Jungle trapdoors work really well as they have a circular cut-out, but it doesn't matter as the brightness will be unaltered by the trapdoors.

SOFA

Minecraft doesn't have much seating, but you can make an armchair or sofa using stairs and some signs. Simply place the stairs as if they're a bench, then attach blank signs (using the same type of wood) to the sides to form simple armrests. It's super-easy, but looks just like a real sofa!

COMPUTER

Bring Minecraft up to date with a desktop PC. Place stair blocks with the tall edge facing the front of a desk, then put a 1x1 painting on the back of them to form a screen. Now put an activator rail in front to resemble a keyboard. You might have to place two to get the correct orientation, but simply break the one you don't need!

TIP: Make a planter by surrounding one block of dirt with trapdoors.

HOW TO...
BREW THE BEST POTIONS

Brewing potions is a great way to level up your skills and make yourself even stronger. Here are the best ones you can make!

POTION OF STRENGTH

Prepping for a fight? Brew blaze powder into an awkward potion to make a Potion of Strength, which gives you 1.5 extra attack points for three minutes. Add redstone dust to extend the potion's duration to eight minutes, or glowstone dust to add three attack points (but just for one and a half minutes).

AWKWARD POTION

The awkward potion is the base for almost ALL useful potions. You can brew one by filtering Nether wart into a water bottle using a brewing stand powered by blaze powder. Brew the ingredients on these pages into an awkward potion first, otherwise you'll end up with something completely useless!

POTION OF HEALING

Probably the most useful potion! Brew a glistering melon slice (crafted from gold nuggets surrounding a melon slice) into an awkward potion to get 4 points of health restored when you drink it. Add glowstone dust to the potion to get 8 points when you drink it!

TIP: Fermented spider eyes can alter a potion's effects in surprising ways.

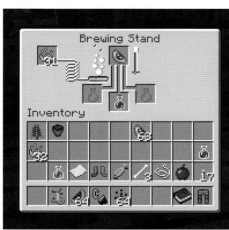

SPLASH POTION OF HARMING

Adding a fermented spider eye (craft sugar and a spider eye) to a Potion of Healing will create a Potion of Harming, although in this state it's not much use because if you drink it you'll lose health. However, add some gunpowder to turn it into a splash Potion of Harming that can be thrown as a weapon. Add glowstone dust to power it up, and at its strongest point it will do almost 12 points of damage.

POTION OF NIGHT VISION

Seeing in the dark can flip the advantage in your favour. Craft a golden carrot (surround a carrot with gold nuggets), then brew it into an awkward potion for three minutes of Night Vision. Add redstone dust to extend it for eight minutes!

TIP: Other items to use in brewing include sugar, a rabbit's foot, ghast tears, magma cream, turtle shells and phantom membranes.

POTION OF WATER BREATHING

Brew a pufferfish into an awkward potion, then add redstone dust to create a Potion of Water Breathing, which lasts for eight whole minutes, meaning you won't lose any oxygen while you're beneath the surface. A few of these are essential for tackling ocean monuments!

HOW TO...
CRAFT AMAZING
FIREWORKS

There are millions of different firework combinations you can make, so it's time to get started!

ROCKETS

A basic firework is made by combining a rocket and at least one firework star, although a firework can have up to seven stars! A rocket is made from one paper and up to three gunpowder. Place a rocket on the ground, and it will shoot into the air and explode. The more gunpowder, the higher it will go, but without a firework star the explosion will be empty. If you add a firework star, it will show the effects of the star when it explodes.

FIREWORK STARS

A simple firework star is made of one gunpowder and one piece of dye. This creates a small ball explosion in the colour of the dye you use. However, adding more dyes makes the firework's effect fade from one dye to another after it has exploded. You can also add one shape modifier and either of the effects modifiers. Since you can add up to seven firework stars to one firework, it's easy to craft some complicated and varied fireworks!

TIP: You can also use fireworks as a boost when flying with elytra.

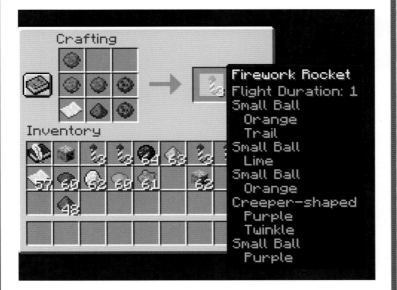

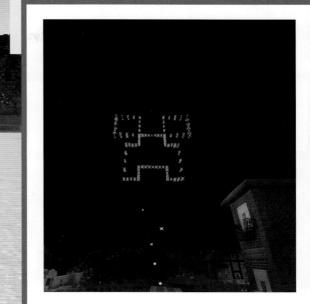

SHAPE MODIFIERS

The standard shape of a firework is a small ball, but this can be changed by adding certain items to the firework star. Only one shape modifier is allowed per firework star, although you can have several in one firework. A fire charge makes a large ball explosion. A gold nugget makes a star-shaped explosion. Adding any mob head will make an explosion in the shape of a creeper face, and a feather makes a starburst explosion.

EFFECTS MODIFIERS

As well as changing the shape of an explosion, you can use a modifier to change the style of it. Glowstone dust makes the particles crackle as they fade away, and diamonds make the particles leave trails behind them. Unlike shape modifiers, you can add both of these to a star – if there's room!

DAMAGE

A firework explosion doesn't damage blocks, but can cause up to 5 points of damage if it explodes close to a player or mob. You can load a rocket into a crossbow by placing it in your offhand slot, and these rockets will do 5-6 points of damage plus 1-2 per firework star, for a maximum of 18 damage!

TIP: Using a rocket in a crossbow does three points of durability damage per shot.

HOW TO...
ACTIVATE A
CONDUIT

Conduits give you underwater protection. If you've never made one, here's how simple it is!

COLLECTING MATERIALS

Conduits are made up of some fairly rare materials, so collecting them will likely take you a long time! You'll need to find eight nautilus shells, which can be obtained as a treasure item while fishing, in some underwater treasure chests, by trading with wandering traders and by killing a drowned that's holding one. You also need one heart of the sea – there's one in every buried treasure chest, which you can find using a map from a shipwreck. Finally, you need up to 42 prismarine-type blocks, which you can get from monuments, or craft by collecting prismarine shards from guardians.

EFFECTS

Why would you want to build a conduit? The main reason is because when you're close to one, you NEVER run out of oxygen, so you can stay underwater to build or explore for longer periods of time. Conduits also give off a bright light AND imbue nearby players with Underwater Night Vision, so you can see mobs coming as well as what's around you. Conduit power also increases your underwater mining speed, which is ideal for tackling monuments. And last but not least, when a full frame is built, the conduit will damage any mobs that come within eight blocks!

TIP: Almost any type of prismarine works in a conduit, but not partial blocks like stairs, slabs and walls.

CONDUIT BLOCK

To make a conduit block, which lies at the centre of a conduit structure, you need to place a heart of the sea on a crafting table, then surround it with eight nautilus shells. You can now place this block anywhere in the water to begin building a conduit. As well as giving out light level 15, it will emit conduit power in every direction once you start building the frame. Conduits can be placed on land, but will have no effect – they have to be surrounded by water to work.

CONDUIT FRAMES

The prismarine you collected is used to power up the conduit frame, similar to bookshelves for an enchanting table. Place the prismarine blocks at a one-block gap from the conduit, and every seven blocks (from a minimum of 16 to a maximum of 42) will increase the range slightly. A complete frame consists of a ring of blocks in all three directions, as shown opposite. The area inside the frame must be filled with water!

TIP: When a conduit frame is full, the range extends across 96 blocks.

21 EXPLO TIPS

If you're trying to conquer the world (in Minecraft!), here's what you need to remember...

5 FISH IN THE RAIN FOR BETTER CATCHES

1 Minecarts are usually slower than sprinting, but you can also use the time spent riding in them to organise and craft.

2 If you don't like the rain, remember you can sleep in a bed during a storm to skip it.

3 Pumpkins can't be eaten, but craft them with sugar and an egg to make pumpkin pie.

4 While riding a horse or sprinting, you can cross one-block gaps without stopping.

5 Fish in open water while it's raining for the best chance of catching good items.

6 Walking up and down stairs uses less energy than jumping up and down slopes, so always install some stairs if you make regular trips to high or low places.

7 Always place torches on the same side of a cave so you can find your way back easily.

8 Use lily pads to make simple bridges – you can walk over them.

9 Always remember to store your stuff regularly while exploring underground – that way, if you die, you don't lose too much.

10 Take care when mining underwater, as it will create a downward suction current that might trap you.

11 Never break the block you're standing on, as you've got no idea if it hides a long drop or a lava lake, or something equally deadly!

RATION

12 Look out for azalea trees, as they mark the position of Lush Caves biomes.

13 Wood is rare underground, but you can grow trees by planting saplings in dirt, then using bone meal on them, as long as there's enough space.

14 Bunny-hopping (sprinting and jumping) is slightly quicker than just sprinting, but also more exhausting!

15 It's impossible to fall off a block while you're sneaking.

16 Carry a bed with you to skip nights, but remember that if you die and your last-used bed isn't there, you return to the world spawn point.

17 Cobblestone, wood planks and iron ingots are the three most useful items in the game, so make sure you've always got a good supply of them all.

18 Take care when breaking the walls in igloo basements – like strongholds, the stone brick blocks can hide monster eggs full of silverfish.

8 USE LILY PADS AS A BRIDGE

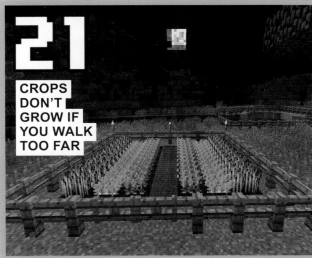

15 SNEAKING STOPS YOU FALLING OFF BLOCKS

21 CROPS DON'T GROW IF YOU WALK TOO FAR

19 The Mushroom Fields biome is one of the safest – no hostile mobs spawn there, even underground!

20 The day-night cycle takes 20 minutes to complete, and mobs can only spawn for the darkest seven minutes of night.

21 Crops don't grow if you walk too far away from them.

HOW TO...
CREATE MINECART
RAILWAYS

Minecart railways can be used for transporting goods, mobs or yourself long distances!

RAILS

All minecarts run on rails, otherwise they don't run very far! The simplest kind of rails can be crafted from six iron ingots and a stick, although it's also possible to collect them from abandoned mines, which house a huge number of tracks, and you'll find plenty inside loot chests. Collecting them is a lot easier than crafting them, so fill your pockets when you stumble over some!

REDSTONE RAILS

Several types of rail can interact with redstone power:
Activator rails are crafted from six iron ingots, two sticks and a redstone torch. When powered, they "activate" any cart that passes over them (e.g. by knocking a rider out of a minecart, or priming a TNT minecart).
Detector rails are crafted from six iron ingots, a stone pressure plate and one redstone dust. They send out a redstone pulse when a minecart passes over them, so you can use a minecart to trigger further circuits.
Powered rails are crafted from six gold ingots, a stick and one redstone dust. They give a minecart a speed boost (when powered) or stop a moving minecart in its tracks (if unpowered).

TIP: Mobs will avoid walking on rails – for their own safety!

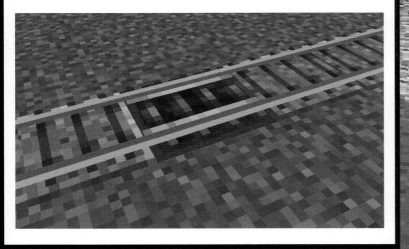

COMBINATION MINECARTS

As well as empty minecarts, you can craft combination minecarts with special abilities. A chest minecart allows you to transport the contents of a chest in a minecart. A hopper minecart lets you funnel a few items in and out of a minecart into or from other areas. TNT minecarts can be rigged to explode, and in the Java Edition a furnace minecart can be fed with coal to slowly push other minecarts.

TIP: If you pass through a gap that's too small while in a minecart, you can take one point of damage.

MINECARTS

To transport something using rails, you have to put it in a minecart. Minecarts will travel on rails if pushed, powered or nudged onto a downhill slope. All minecarts can be placed on rails to move, and be removed from rails by a brief attack, or if they take damage. You can get into a minecart by using it or place a mob into a minecart by pushing them into place. At full speed, a minecart can travel eight blocks a second in any direction, which is about half as fast again as walking speed.

HOW TO...

USE A

COMMAND BLOCK

Command blocks are some of the most powerful tools in the game once you know how to use them...

GETTING COMMAND BLOCKS

Command blocks can be used to execute a console command automatically when a certain condition is met. They can't be obtained in Survival mode, and they're not even in the creative inventory, but in the Java Edition and on tablets and smartphones you can use the console to put one in your inventory by typing /give @p minecraft:command_block

You can place a command block like any other block, but once placed they can't be broken except in Creative mode. Pistons can't move them, and even TNT won't blow them up!

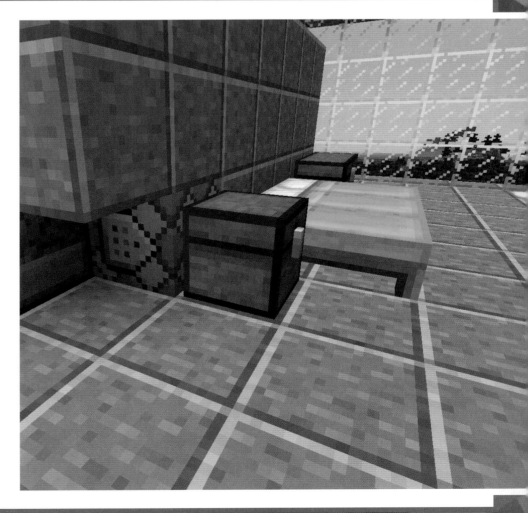

SETTING A COMMAND

Switch to Creative mode, and you can open the GUI by using a command block. Here, you can set the command a block will perform when triggered. Any valid console command should work – for example, you could enter the command /time set day so the command block sets the time to daylight when triggered by a redstone charge. Place a button on the side, and when it's pressed night will turn to day!

TIP: Command blocks aren't available on the console editions.

DEBUGGING

If a command block doesn't do what you want, there's probably an error in the command. To check what's going on, open the GUI and look at the previous output box. If there was an error message, it will appear here. You can place a redstone comparator next to a command block, and it will read the output value and create a redstone signal with a strength based on whether the command worked or not.

COMMAND BLOCK TYPES

Command blocks can be set to three modes. An orange block is an impulse block, meaning it activates once when redstone power triggers it. A purple block is a repeating block, meaning it activates once per game tick (20 times a second) and you can set it to require power or not. A green block is a chain block, which only activates once a previously linked command block has completed its command. All types of block can be set to need redstone power or not.

TIP: Command blocks can be linked together to make very complicated circuits – try it out!

HOW TO...
BARTER WITH PIGLINS

The inhabitants of the Nether aren't necessarily upset to see you, as long as you bring gifts!

PIGLINS

Piglins spawn in Nether Wastes and Crimson Forest biomes. They're equipped with a crossbow or sword and will attack you on sight unless you're wearing at least one piece of golden armour. This is because they LOVE gold! A piglin has 16 health points and an attack power of 2-13 points, depending on the difficulty level and attack type used.

BARTERING

Piglins don't trade like villagers – instead, they barter. To do this, you have to throw a gold ingot on the ground near a piglin and wait while they inspect it. They'll respond by dropping, in order of most to least rare, 8-16 blackstone, 6-12 gravel, 2-8 arrows, 2-8 Nether bricks, 2-8 soul sand, 2-4 leather, a fire charge, 1-3 crying obsidian, obsidian, 5-12 Nether quartz, 3-9 string, 2-4 ender pearls, 10-36 iron nuggets, a water bottle, a Potion of Fire Resistance, a splash Potion of Fire Resistance, enchanted iron boots or an enchanted book.

TIP: Even if you're wearing gold armour, piglins may attack if they hear you open a chest or you mine some gold-containing blocks nearby.

HOSTILE PIGLINS

Piglin brutes, which carry axes and live in Bastion Remnants, can't be bartered with. If you bring a piglin to the Overworld, it will survive for just 15 seconds before turning into a zombified piglin. When this happens, it will drop any items it has collected, although its armour can still be worn while it's a zombie.

GOLD ITEMS

Piglins will collect any gold or gold-containing item they spot. If they collect gold armour or weapons, they'll equip them, assuming they're not already equipped with something better. This doesn't count as bartering, because they drop nothing in return, but it does distract them, which is useful if you plan to attack!

SCARING PIGLINS

Piglins can be easily scared. They'll run away from soul fire or any soul fire item (such as a soul campfire or soul lantern). They'll also retreat from zombified piglins if they get too close. Baby piglins are rare because they never grow into adult piglins. They also can't be bartered with and are scared of wither skeletons and withers.

HOW TO... FORM A WOLF PACK

The best fights are the ones you don't even have to have - and a tame wolf can help you out here!

FINDING WOLVES

Wild wolves can spawn in any Taiga or Forest biome, except Flower Forests. They initially spawn in packs of four, with one in three packs containing a puppy. Wolves are neutral to begin with and don't attack the player if attacked themselves, though if you injure one wolf the entire pack will turn on you, so be careful!

TAMING WOLVES

To tame a wolf, you simply have to feed it bones. Each bone has a one in three chance of taming the wolf. When a wolf is tamed, it will receive a red collar and its health will increase from 8 to 20 points. It will also start to follow you around, unless you've told it to sit. By taming multiple wolves, you can form a whole pack! Wolves bred from tamed parents will also be loyal to the same player as their parents.

TIP: If you stray more than 12 blocks from a tame wolf and it hasn't been told to sit, it will teleport close to you.

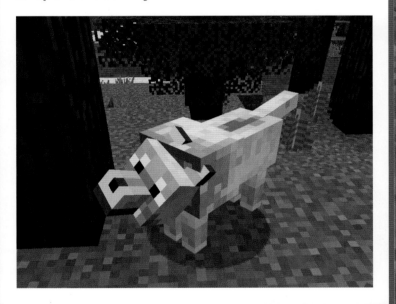

FOOD

You can breed wolves by feeding them any type of meat, including rotten flesh and raw chicken. In fact, this makes it a great way to use up rotten flesh! Feeding almost any meat food item to a wolf will replenish its health to some extent, and in the Bedrock Edition you can also feed them all types of fish and rabbit stew. Wolves can't get food poisoning and will enter love mode if fed while already at full health.

TIP: Personalise your wolf pack by using dye on their collars to change the colour from red.

PACK ATTACKS

On most modern editions of Minecraft, there's no limit to the number of wolves you can tame, although the higher the number, the less manageable your pack will become! Tamed wolves will attack anything that attacks them or the player in groups, so the more you have, the deadlier your pack becomes! The attack strength of a tame wolf is 4 points, while the attack strength of wild wolves varies from 3-6 points depending on the difficulty level in-game.

HOW TO...
CONTROL A LLAMA

Llamas can be tamed and used to carry huge numbers of items, but only if you know how to control them....

WHERE TO FIND LLAMAS

Llamas spawn in two biomes: Savanna Plateaus and Mountains. They're usually found in groups of four or five, and although they fight back by spitting if attacked, they're mostly neutral. Each llama has 15-30 points of health, and can have brown, cream, grey or white skin. Wandering traders spawn with two llamas in tow!

TAMING LLAMAS

You can tame a llama the same way as a horse: get on its back by clicking use while your hand is empty, then wait until you're thrown off. Repeat the process until hearts rise from its head, signifying that the llama is tame. Unfortunately, you can't control a llama while riding on it – you need to use a lead (craftable from four string and one slimeball). Putting a llama on a lead will allow you to pull it close behind you.

TIP: Llamas drop two pieces of leather when killed, as well as any items they're carrying.

BREEDING LLAMAS

Feeding a hay bale to a llama will put it into breeding mode, and you can use further hay bales to speed up the growth of a baby llama. The baby llama will have an equal chance of taking either of its parents' fur colours. Each llama has a secret strength value of between one and five, which determines how many items it can carry, and baby llamas randomly have a strength value of between one and its strongest parent's strength value. Only one in 60 llamas has a full strength value of five.

CARAVANS

The cool thing about llamas is you can turn them into a caravan to carry goods across long distances. If you put a tame llama on a leash, other nearby llamas will get in line behind it. The llamas will then all follow the one in front as you lead it around. Equip each llama with a chest, and the caravan can transport 150 items (15 items per llama) plus 10 chests and 10 pieces of carpet. A single carpet tile can be placed on the back of a llama to decorate it – each colour of tile has a different decoration.

21 COMBAT TIPS

Combat is a major part of Minecraft, so here's how you can attack and defend like an expert!

1
WATER BLOCKS CREEPER EXPLOSIONS

1 Water blocks the effects of a creeper explosion, so you can hide in it to stay safe.

2 On higher difficulty levels, mobs are more powerful if they spawn during a full moon.

3 Blazes drop 10 experience, which is higher than almost all other normal mobs.

4 When fighting a witch, use a bucket of milk to negate their potion attacks.

5 Undead mobs burn in direct sunlight, but they can survive in water or by hiding in the shade.

6 Gold horse armour is uniquely stronger than its iron counterpart.

7 You can hook a mob with a fishing rod, but this will remove 5 durability from the tool.

8 Chainmail armour can't be crafted, only collected from mobs or traded for with a blacksmith villager.

9 You can halve the range at which a mob will become hostile towards you by wearing a mob head as a helmet.

10 The "score" you see when you die is a reflection of how much experience you've collected since you last died.

11 Axes do more damage than swords in a single hit, but lose durability faster and are slower to recover for another strike.

12 To make a critical hit with a sword, jump and then attack

8 CHAINMAIL CAN'T BE CRAFTED

11 AXES DO MORE DAMAGE THAN SWORDS

18 TURTLE HELMETS HAVE ARMOUR POINTS

with your sword as you're falling towards the ground.

 The damage done by crossbows varies, but at their strongest they do 11 points of damage per hit.

 Tridents can't be crafted or bought – only collected from drowned.

15 Leather armour has low protection, but wearing even one piece will stop you freezing in powder snow.

16 Tridents do more damage when used as a melee weapon than when thrown.

17 It takes 24 units of any viable material to make a full set of armour.

18 Wearing pumpkins or mob heads doesn't offer any armour protection, although a turtle shell worn as a helmet does have armour points.

19 Golden items offer higher level enchantments than those made of

other materials, although they wear out a lot quicker too!

20 Bows can fire 385 arrows before they break – that's six inventory stacks of arrows.

21 You can place a specific stack of arrows in your offhand slot to ensure those are used as ammo.

HOW TO...
SUMMON
THE WITHER

Minecraft's scariest foe - made all the more terrifying because you chose to summon it...

INTO THE NETHER

You can't summon a wither without first collecting items from the Nether. That means building a Nether portal, or repairing a ruined one! In either case, you need obsidian, which can only be gathered using a diamond pickaxe and forms where water flows over lava source blocks. Build a portal frame that's no less than four obsidian blocks wide and six obsidian blocks high, so it has at least a 2x3 gap inside, then ignite the portal using a flint & steel on the inside of that gap. You can repair a ruined portal by filling in the missing blocks and replacing any crying obsidian with regular obsidian, then igniting it the same way.

SOUL SAND

To build the wither's totem, which allows you to summon it, you need to collect soul soil or soul sand. Soul soil is found only in the Soul Sand Valley biome (the one with blue flames and large fossils), while soul sand is found near the lower reaches of the Nether in the Nether Wastes biome and in Nether fortresses. The fastest way to collect it is with a shovel, and you need four blocks per totem.

TIP: You can summon the wither in any dimension, even the Nether or the End!

WITHER SKULLS

The last thing you need to build the wither's totem is three wither skeleton skulls. These are dropped by wither skeletons when they're killed, but only one in 40 kills will result in one, on average. That means you'll have to slay around 120 wither skeletons to collect the correct number of skulls. Wither skeletons are found only in Nether fortresses in the Nether, so you'll have to find one AND survive long enough to collect their heads!

SUMMON THE WITHER

The wither's totem is fairly simple to build – place four blocks of soul sand or soul soil in a T shape, then place the three wither skeleton skulls on top. Note that you have to place the skulls last, and you can't be in Peaceful mode, otherwise the wither will fail to appear. If you've done it correctly, the totem will turn into a wither and flash white – at this point, run away! When the wither arrives, there's going to be a huge explosion, and you don't want to be anywhere near it. Good luck with the fight!

TIP: It's possible to summon multiple withers at once – not that it's a good idea!

HOW TO...
BEAT EVERY MOB

Every mob in Minecraft has a secret, and knowing what these are will help you defeat them!

■ **Baby zombies** don't burn in sunlight, and are faster than normal zombies.
■ **Blazes** take damage from snowballs, as well as the knockback other mobs experience.
■ **Cave spiders** inflict the Poison effect with their bites.
■ **Creepers** run away from cats and ocelots.
■ **Drowned** will turn into normal zombies if lured onto land for 30 seconds.
■ **Endermen** take damage from water – including rain!
■ **Endermites** suffocate if they walk on soul sand.
■ **Evokers** have a five-second cooldown

CAVE SPIDERS INFLICT POISON

on summoning fangs and a 17-second cooldown on summoning vexes.

▪ **Ghasts** can spot you from 100 blocks away. Their attacks can't destroy stone blocks.

▪ **Guardian** laser attacks can't be dodged.

▪ **Hoglins** will not be provoked if you kill a nearby baby hoglin.

▪ **Husks** don't burn in sunlight and will inflict Hunger if they bite you.

▪ **Magma cubes** spawn in groups of up to five in Basalt Deltas.

▪ **Phantoms** only attack players who haven't slept for three days or more.

TIP: Ravagers drop the most experience of any Overworld mob – 20 points per kill!

HUSKS DON'T BURN IN SUNLIGHT

RAVAGERS TAKE LESS KNOCKBACK

▪ **Piglins** can be distracted briefly by gold items.

▪ **Ravagers** take 50% less knockback from attacks because of their size.

▪ **Shulkers** teleport away if they come into contact with water.

▪ **Silverfish** will heal if they return to hiding inside a block.

▪ **Skeletons** don't burn in sunlight if they're wearing a helmet or wading in water.

▪ **Slimes** don't spawn close to players, even in swampland biomes.

▪ **Spiders** can't climb up ice blocks.

▪ **Spider jockeys** and **Chicken jockeys** can be forced to separate if you knock them into water.

▪ **Strays** shoot arrows tipped with Slowness.

▪ **Vexes** look like ghosts but aren't technically undead mobs, so use a splash Potion of Harming, not Healing!

▪ **Vindicators** won't follow you through an iron door.

▪ **Witches** are naturally 85% resistant to damage from enchantments and potions.

▪ **Wither skeletons** are scared away by wolves, including tame wolves.

▪ **Zombies** can break down wooden doors on higher difficulty modes.

▪ **Zombified piglins** can replace their weapon with any better one they find.

TIP: Endermen are the only mob to appear in all three dimensions – the Overworld, the Nether and the End!

WITCHES RESIST DAMAGE FROM POTIONS

HOW TO...
TAME A
FOX

Although shy and harmless, a fox can be a useful ally, if you can only gain its trust....

WHERE TO FIND FOXES

Foxes spawn in Taiga, Giant Tree Taiga and Snowy Taiga biomes, and can be found in groups of 2-4 animals. They're nocturnal, so they try to sleep during the day and move around at night. They'll attempt to sleep in shade, usually under a tree or in a small cave. At night, they'll search nearby villages for food. Foxes that spawn in the snowy biome are entirely white but otherwise identical to the standard orange fox.

FOX BEHAVIOUR

Wild foxes can be quite damaging to tame mob populations – left uncontrolled, they'll pounce on chickens, rabbits, cod, salmon, tropical fish and baby turtles, and try to kill them. If you gain their trust, however, they'll leave those mobs alone and come to your aid if you're attacked. Sleeping foxes will wake up if the light level where they're resting raises or they're approached by a player or mob.

TIP: Foxes never attack wolves or polar bears, even if that mobs attacks them.

TAMING A FOX

Although foxes will automatically run away from players if approached, you can use the sneak button to get near to them. When you get close enough, you can feed foxes a sweet berry to put them into breeding mode. If you breed two foxes to create a baby fox, that fox will be tame and trust you. Unfortunately, adult foxes can never be tamed! If an orange fox breeds with an arctic fox, the baby has a random chance of being either colour.

The good news is sweet berries grow in Taiga biomes, so it's easy to collect the necessary fruit. Sweet berries can also be fed to baby foxes to help speed up their growth.

FOX GIFTS

One in five adult foxes spawns holding an item from a list of emeralds, rabbit's foot, rabbit hide, egg, wheat, leather, and feather. They have a normal chance to drop these items when killed, but will also put them down to attack. Trusting foxes may, from time to time, turn up with gifts for the player.

TIP: Sweet berry bushes are spiky and will hurt if you walk through them, although they don't affect foxes in this way!

HOW TO...

SPEEDRUN MINECRAFT

Believe it or not, Minecraft DOES have an ending, and here's how you can get to it quickly!

PREPARING

Even a speedrun needs the basics taken care of; a good food supply (a stack of cooked steaks should do it!), a bow and plenty of arrows, and some decent tools and armour are a must. If you collect enough wood to craft pickaxes and dig for diamonds as quickly as you can, you should be able to find plenty, collecting coal and iron along the way. A base with a bed is also a must – you're almost definitely going to die while attempting this run!

The most important thing is to collect as many ender pearls as possible. Aim for around 30 before you set out on the next step.

VISITING THE NETHER

Build a Nether portal. You can collect obsidian with a diamond pickaxe underground, or dump water over lava source blocks to create it at surface level. You need a minimum of 10 to make a Nether portal, but taking another 10 with you will make returning easier! You need to find a Nether fortress and kill blazes to collect blaze rods. Each rod makes two blaze powder, so you need half as many rods as you have ender pearls. Once you hit that number, it's back to the Overworld!

TIP: Eating golden apples gives you Fire Resistance – useful against blazes!

LOCATING A STRONGHOLD

Craft your blaze powder and pearls into eyes of ender, and now it's time to find a stronghold. Throw the eyes of ender and follow the trails they leave until they start hovering in one place. Dig down to find the entrance to a stronghold. It makes sense to establish a small base and set a spawn point at the start of a stronghold, as things are about to get really tough!

REACHING THE END

Locate the End portal room and activate it. You need up to 11 eyes of ender to activate an End portal, so hold onto that number at least! Once you've activated the portal, it's time to hit the End. Remember this is a one-way trip unless you beat the dragon, so don't go in unless you're fully equipped for a fight! Plenty of arrows are a must, as are healing items.

KILLING THE DRAGON

Easier said than done, perhaps, but use arrows to break the ender crystals first, and think about wearing a pumpkin head to avoid provoking endermen. Poison effects won't hurt the dragon, so don't waste time trying them! Once you kill the dragon, jump through the exit portal and you're finished!

TIP: Take empty glass bottles to the End to collect dragon's breath.

HOW TO...
BUILD AN END PORTAL

Sick of trying to find an End portal? Here's how you can build your own in Creative mode!

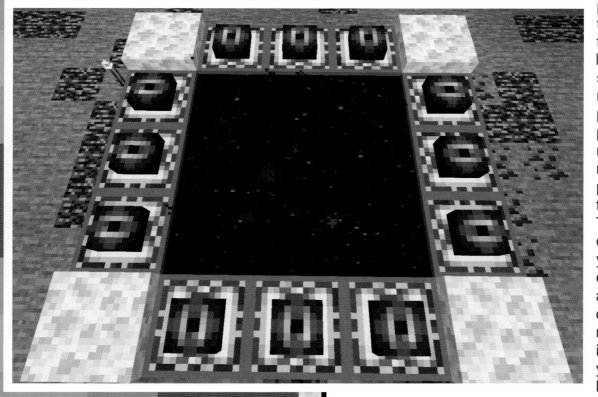

MATERIALS

■ **End portal frame blocks:** These blocks can't be obtained except in the creative inventory – the ones that generate in the game are indestructible! You need 12 to make an End portal.

■ **Eyes of ender:** Also available in the creative inventory, but can be crafted from blaze powder and ender pearls. When placed in a correctly built portal frame, they activate the End portal.

■ **Corner-stones:** While not technically part of the portal, you need some material to place the portal frames against. This can be dirt or sand if you want to clear it away afterwards, or something more elaborate if you want your portal to look cool!

LOCATION

In the place where you want to build your portal, place four cornerstones in a square with three blocks of space between them. The material the corners are made of doesn't matter, but you'll need to stand in the middle of the square to place the portal blocks. You can build an End portal in any location including the Nether, but once you activate it anything inside the portal frame will be permanently deleted.

TIP: You can break portal blocks in Creative mode.

CONSTRUCTION

Portal blocks can be placed in several orientations, so you need to get this bit right. Stand in the centre of the square and place three portal blocks into the gaps between each cornerstone. The green line should be pointing towards where you're standing. If you've done it correctly, you should have placed 12 blocks to create a 3x3 space around you (see the screenshots to make sure you did it right!).

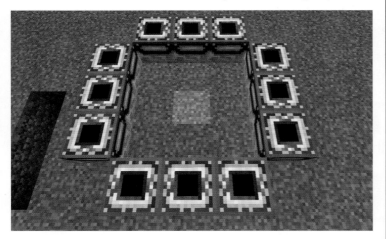

ACTIVATION

If you've built the frame correctly, you can place the eyes of ender into the frame blocks to activate the portal. If you're still standing inside the frame when it activates, you'll immediately be transported to the End, so take care! If you built your frame in the End, it will work like an exit portal – useful because it works even if you haven't killed the dragon yet!

TIP: Once you activate the portal, breaking the frame won't deactivate it!

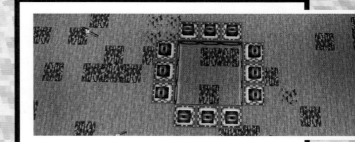

TROUBLESHOOTING

If the portal didn't activate like in this screenshot, consider these solutions:
■ Have you put all 12 eyes of ender into the portal frame?
■ Are the portal blocks oriented correctly? The green stripes should point to the centre, and when the eye of ender is in the block, the white shine on the eye should be on the outside of the frame.
■ Is the portal definitely the right size? You need 12 portal blocks.

21 EXPERT TIPS

Ready to play like the best? Here are some of the tips and secrets only the best players know...

1 Place a beacon near your base to give yourself extra powers and abilities.

2 Create an infinite water source by placing two water source blocks diagonally from one another in a 2x2 hole.

3 Force a sapling to grow tall for extra wood by planting it in a three-block deep hole.

4 You can heal injured villagers by trading with them or using a splash Potion of Healing.

5 Cauldrons can fill up with rain (or snow!) if you leave them outdoors.

6 Some blocks, like beds and hay, will cushion a fall slightly, doing less damage.

7 Throw ender pearls to teleport down long drops to avoid damage.

2

INFINITE WATER

8 Axes aren't just for chopping down trees – they break almost all wood-based blocks quickly.

9 You can survive long drops by landing in water, which stops you from taking any damage.

10 Lava buckets can power a furnace for 12 times longer than one piece of coal.

11 Shearing a sheep makes it drop more wool than killing it does – three blocks instead of one.

12 Planting crops in alternating rows (e.g. potatoes next to radishes) means they grow faster.

6 HAY BREAKS YOUR FALL

12 PLANT CROPS IN ROWS

13 Try not to waste food – you can't overfill your hunger bar. Cookies restore one point of health each, so use those to top up instead of more filling foods.

14 When powering up an enchanting table, bookshelves will only have an effect up to the 15th – after that it's just for decoration.

15 Crafting items into resource blocks (e.g. diamonds into a diamond block) is reversible, so it allows you to essentially carry 576 items in one inventory slot (one stack of 64 blocks, with nine pieces per block).

16 You can combine similar low-level enchantments on an item or book to level up the enchantment (e.g. combine two Sharpness I books to create one Sharpness II book).

17 When crafting a golem or building the wither's totem, you always have to place the heads last.

18 Leave some crops for villagers – they can harvest and replant them if you do.

19 THE SUN SETS IN THE WEST

19 Just like in the real world, the sun in Minecraft rises in the East and sets in the West, so check out its position and whether it's rising or setting to orient yourself.

20 You can mine blocks from a distance of around four blocks away.

21 Obsidian's the strongest breakable block. It takes 250 seconds to break by hand!

HOW TO...
USE COPPER

The newest material in Minecraft, copper can be used in loads of cool ways!

CREATING COPPER

Like other metals, copper is found as ore, collected as raw materials, then smelted into ingots. Copper ingots can be used to craft different items, including copper blocks, slabs and stairs. Copper can also be crafted into a few items, although unlike iron and gold it isn't suitable for tools and armour – at least, not yet!

OXIDISATION

The main difference between copper and other metals is that, like in real life, copper tarnishes over time, turning from orange-bronze to blue-green. The oxidisation process is random and depends on proximity to other copper blocks, but starts after 20 minutes. There are four visible stages – completely unweathered (completely bronze), exposed (mostly bronze), weathered (mostly green), and oxidised (completely green). You can de-oxidise copper by one level using the axe's alternate function on it.

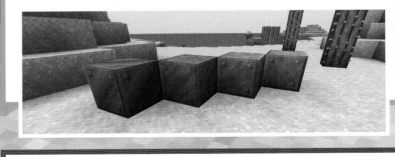

WAXING

By crafting a copper block with honeycomb collected from a beehive or nest, it's possible to wax copper, which protects it from further oxidisation and locks it at its current state. You need to use one piece of honeycomb per block. You can remove wax from a copper block by using the axe's alternate function on it.

TIP: Waxed blocks can be crafted back into ingots, losing the wax.

CUT COPPER

Crafting four copper blocks together will create four cut copper blocks. Cut copper can be turned into slabs or stairs, and will retain its current level of oxidisation and/or waxing. Stairs and slabs can't be waxed after they're crafted. It's also possible to use a stonecutter to turn individual copper blocks into stairs and slabs.

LIGHTNING ROD

Crafted from several copper ingots, a lightning rod can attract a lightning strike during a storm, either to protect flammable structures from being set alight, to utilise the strike's transformative power (e.g. to turn a creeper into a charged creeper), or to use as a redstone trigger. Lightning rods can also be protective – they override the lightning strike target created by a trident with the Channelling enchantment.

SPYGLASS

Using an amethyst shard (collected from a geode) and two copper ingots, you can craft a spyglass, which will allow you to zoom in on things in the distance. Peering through a spyglass slows you down and can only be done for one minute at a time before you lower the spyglass.

TIP: Unwaxed copper will be completely deoxidised if struck by lightning.

HOW TO... MAKE A TURTLE HELMET

MATERIALS

To craft a turtle shell, you need nothing but turtle scutes, but getting hold of them is difficult! Turtles drop one scute when they grow from their baby form into an adult form, so the easiest way to get them is to breed turtles. Be prepared for plenty of waiting around!

> The turtle shell might make a solid weapon in some computer games, but in Minecraft it's a great piece of headgear!

TURTLE FARMING

First, find a group of turtles on a beach somewhere. Fence them off so they can't swim too far away, then feed them seagrass to make them enter love mode. The turtle will return to its home beach (hopefully the one you found it on!) and lay 1-4 eggs.

WEARING THE HELMET

When placed in the head slot of your armour inventory, a turtle shell appears to be worn on the head like a helmet. It gives the player two armour points – the same as a golden, iron or chainmail helmet – absorbing 8% of damage inflicted. More usefully, it also inflicts the Water Breathing status effect so that you have 10 seconds of additional oxygen while underwater.

HATCHING TURTLES

Turtle eggs take 4-5 in-game days to hatch, and grow fastest at night. Zombies and zombie variants will try to destroy them by walking on them, so make sure you protect them and stay clear of the eggs yourself! When they hatch, the baby turtles will head for water and take about 20 minutes to grow into an adult. **TIP: Feed a baby turtle seagrass to speed up the time it takes to grow by 10%.**

ENCHANTMENTS

The turtle shell can receive several enchantments: Blast Protection, Fire Protection, Projectile Protection and Protection. It can also take Aqua Affinity, Respiration, Unbreaking, Thorns and Mending, but the last two can only be applied using enchanted books and an anvil.

TIP: A turtle shell can also be brewed into an awkward potion to create a Potion of the Turtle Master, which inflicts both Slowness and Protection effects.

CRAFTING

To make a turtle shell, craft five scutes in the shape of a helmet. A turtle helmet has 276 durability, and you can combine two damaged shells on a crafting table to repair them, gaining a 5% durability bonus for the combined item. You can also partially repair an individual helmet using scutes and an anvil.

HOW TO... REPAIR ANY ITEM

When your gear starts getting old, don't throw it away - see if you can patch it up instead!

DURABILITY

Items that can wear out show a durability bar. This decreases with one use, though it can be decreased further by improper use. Durability of tools, weapons and armour can be decided by the type of material they're crafted from. In ascending order, from least to most durable, the materials go gold, wood, stone, iron, diamond, Netherite. A gold pickaxe has 32 durability, a Netherite one has 2031.

SIMPLE REPAIR

To repair any item with durability, place two partially worn versions of the same material on a crafting grid or grindstone. This gives them the combined durability of both items, plus a 5% bonus of the item's total durability – so combining two diamond pickaxes with 1 durability each would give you a new pickaxe with a durability of just over 100 (1 plus 1 plus 5% of 2031). Repairing items in this way doesn't spend any experience, but it also doesn't carry over enchantments.

Crafting

Diamond Pickaxe

+5 Attack Damage

Inventory

ANVILS

If you want to preserve an enchantment on an item, you can use an anvil to combine it instead. This costs experience, but the repaired item will have its durability restored without losing its existing enchantments. Indeed, you can combine two enchanted items of the same material to combine their enchantments (unless those enchantments exclude one another, like Riptide and Loyalty on a trident).

PATCHING

If you have an item to repair but you don't have a second to combine it with, you can often patch it with some of its original resource by using an anvil. A diamond pickaxe can be repaired with a diamond, for example. These patches restore 25% of an item's durability, which can be inefficient – two iron ingots can make a whole new sword but fix only 50% of a sword's durability – but patching armour is better than crafting new armour, and patching doesn't use as much experience as combining two items!

SMELTING

If you can't repair an item (or don't want to) that doesn't mean you have to throw it away. Almost any wooden item can be burned as fuel for smelting, while metal items can themselves be smelted to recover a gold or iron nugget. It's not much, but it's better than nothing, especially if resources are getting low!

TIP: Although uncraftable, elytra can be repaired using phantom membranes.

HOW TO... FIND NETHERITE

Netherite is the strongest material in the game, so how do you get this amazing metal?

EXCAVATING

You can find raw Netherite in the form of ancient debris, which mostly spawns at low levels in the Nether. To find it, you should explore at levels a few blocks above the lava ocean where it's 10 times more common than anywhere else. However, it can be found in small amounts anywhere above that point. Ancient debris is almost never visible on the surface, and can be found wherever there's Netherrack, basalt or blackstone. Mining ancient debris with a diamond or Netherite pickaxe makes it drop as a block, which you can then smelt into Netherite scrap. This, in turn, can be crafted – four pieces of scrap and four gold ingots make one Netherite ingot.

LOOTING

Both ancient debris and Netherite ingots can be found as loot chest items in bastion remnants. Ingots are found only in the treasure room, while ancient debris can be found in all types of bastion remnant chests but is more common in hoglin stable chests. Bastion remnants are large blackstone fortresses found only in the Nether, and they can occur in any biome except the Basalt Delta.

Tip: Remember you can find gold ore in the Nether, so you don't have to take ingots with you!

OTHER USES

Netherite can be used to craft a lodestone by surrounding an ingot with chiseled stone bricks, which allows you to magnetise a compass to a specific area. You can also craft Netherite ingots into a block of Netherite, which can be used as decoration (admittedly, expensive decoration!) or as storage. Netherite blocks are also valid material for constructing beacon pyramids, and Netherite ingots can power a beacon once you're ready to activate it.

UPGRADING

To make Netherite armour, weapons and tools, you have to take a single Netherite ingot and use it to augment an existing piece of diamond equipment. This can only be done using a smithing table, which is crafted from four wood planks with two iron ingots on top of them. The equipment doesn't need full durability, but the equivalent durability value will be preserved, so it makes sense to start with undamaged items where possible! Netherite armour is unique in looking different to other forms of armour. The tools, however, are the same as any other variety.

Tip: Netherite swords and axes deal more damage than even diamond ones.

HOW TO...
ENCHANT
INCREDIBLE
GEAR

Enchanting helps you take tools to the next level. Here's how to do it and what to look for

HOW TO ENCHANT

First, craft an enchanting table – you need four obsidian, two diamonds and one book. Place the enchanting table in a reasonably large space, then power it by placing up to 15 bookshelves close by – there has to be a one-block gap between the table and the bookshelves. Check the screenshot for more information!

Now, put the item you want to enchant on the table along with up to three pieces of lapis lazuli. You'll be able to select an enchantment from the right-hand list at the cost of some lapis and some experience. If you can't select the enchantment, it may be because you don't have enough experience! There's no way to be sure what enchantment you're selecting, but sometimes you'll get a hint!

ARMOUR ENCHANTMENTS

ARMOUR ENCHANTMENTS

» **Aqua Affinity** – Increases mining speed underwater
» **Blast Protection** – Reduces explosion knockback and damage
» **Depth Strider** – Increases movement speed underwater
» **Feather Falling** – Reduces fall damage
» **Fire Protection** – Reduces fire damage
» **Frost Walker** – Boots turn water into ice
» **Respiration** – Increases breathing time underwater
» **Soul Speed** – Walk faster on soul sand/soil, but lose durability
» **Thorns** – Deal damage to mobs you touch

TIP: To avoid ending up with an enchantment you don't want, enchant a book instead of the tool or item directly.

WEAPON ENCHANTMENTS

» **Bane of Arthropods** – Increases attack damage against spiders and insect mobs
» **Channelling** – Makes a trident channel a bolt of lightning during a storm
» **Fire Aspect** – Sets target on fire
» **Flame** – Sets arrows on fire
» **Impaling** – Tridents deal more damage to ocean mobs

WEAPON ENCHANTMENTS

» **Infinity** – Bows don't consume arrows
» **Knockback** – Weapon does more knockback
» **Looting** – Mobs drop more loot when killed
» **Loyalty** – Trident returns when thrown
» **Multishot** – Crossbows fire three shots per arrow
» **Piercing** – Crossbow arrows travel through targets
» **Power** – Bows do more damage
» **Punch** – Arrows deal more knockback
» **Quick Charge** – Crossbows charge faster
» **Riptide** – Hold onto a trident when thrown (in water)
» **Sharpness** – Swords deal higher damage
» **Smite** – Deal more damage to undead mobs

TOOL ENCHANTMENTS

» **Efficiency** – Increases mining speed
» **Fortune** – Certain blocks drop more items (e.g. ores)

ENCHANTED TOOLS

» **Luck of the Sea** – Better items when fishing
» **Mending** – Experience restores durability
» **Silk Touch** – All mined blocks drop themselves
» **Unbreaking** – Tool loses less durability per use

TIP: Some enchantments, like Frost Walker, can only be obtained as a treasure item.

21 NETHER TIPS

How confident are you when you explore the Nether? With these tips, tricks and secrets, you'll be even better!

1 A RAIL PASSING INTO A PORTAL

1 Minecarts can pass through Nether portals, so you can use them to create interdimensional shortcuts on your railway!

2 Most mobs that spawn in the Nether are immune to fire and lava damage.

3 Water can't exist normally in the Nether, but you can still place it in cauldrons.

4 Snow golems melt in hot biomes, and that includes the Nether!

5 Mobs spawn faster inside Nether fortresses than outside them. You'll never be able to completely empty a fortress.

6 Wither skeletons are the only mob that can drop their own head without being killed by a charged creeper.

7 If you find yourself lost in the Nether, you can quickly return to the Overworld by collecting obsidian and repairing a broken portal.

8 Portals always pick a safe spot to spawn in the Nether and the Overworld, but that doesn't mean they won't spawn on the edge of something dangerous!

9 Any mob can use portals, so it's possible for mobs to wander into the Nether – or wander out!

10 For every block you travel in the Nether, you move eight in the Overworld.

11 Use glowstone and crying obsidian to craft and charge

8

PORTALS ARE
ALWAYS SAFE

11

A RESPAWN
ANCHOR

15

A PIGLIN
BRUTE

a respawn anchor so you can respawn in the Nether.

12 Don't try using a bed in the Nether as it will explode like TNT when you try to sleep in it!

13 Once you have Netherite, place a lodestone by your entry portal so you can find your way back there!

14 Striders can be saddled and ridden – control them with a fungus-on-a-stick.

15 Piglin brutes, found in bastions, have 40 health points and drop 20 experience when killed.

16 Warped (blue) Forests are the safest biome in the Nether – no mobs spawn there except endermen.

17 Magma cubes spawn more frequently in the Basalt Delta biome, so watch out – especially if you're low down!

18 Water, ice and snow will immediately evaporate in the Nether, and wet sponges will dry out as soon as they're placed.

19 Take a bowl to craft mushroom stew for food when you're in the Nether, because mushrooms are abundant there. You can also kill hoglins to collect pork chops.

20 Nether fortresses contain lots of useful loot, as well as blazes and Nether wart, which assist in crafting potions. Keep a note of where you find one!

21 Netherrack breaks very quickly, but beware – this can mean your tools chew through their durability faster than you realise!

HOW TO... CURE A ZOMBIE

Not every zombie is a lost cause. Some can be brought back to life!

ZOMBIE VILLAGERS

Most zombies can transform in some way – zombies turn into drowned in water or husks in the desert, while husks turn into zombies if waterlogged and zombies into drowned if underwater. Zombie villagers, though? They can be turned back into villagers, as long as you know what you're doing. The clue for this is found in igloo basements, which are part of 50% of igloos. Look under the carpet, head down there, and you'll find everything you need to get started, including the zombie!

EQUIPMENT

If you don't have a basement to hand, you can craft everything you need. A golden apple is crafted from eight gold ingots and one apple. A splash Potion of Weakness is brewed by filtering a fermented spider eye and gunpowder into a water bottle (note: NOT an awkward potion). You can also optionally use iron bars (six iron ingots) and a bed (three of the same-coloured wool and three wood planks).

TIP: Remember in Peaceful mode the zombie villager won't spawn in an igloo basement.

FINAL TRANSFORMATION

At this point, you have to wait and hope it's worked! It can take 2-5 minutes for the cure to take full effect, and the zombie will keep attacking while it does. Soon the zombie will begin to shudder, then transform back into a villager, who you can start trading with if you like! Set the villager free and they'll wander off in search of a village. For fun, try to protect them on their journey!

TIP: You can tell the profession of a villager by looking at their outfit.

ADMINISTERING THE CURE

For best results, trap the zombie in a makeshift cell. If you use the bed and iron bars, the process can be sped up slightly, but they aren't required. You're mostly just making sure the zombie doesn't attack you, and that it's safe when it turns back into a villager! Start by throwing the splash Potion of Weakness at the zombie. Small particle swirls will come off it to indicate that the potion has taken effect. Now select the golden apple, and get close enough to feed it to the zombie by pressing the use button. If done correctly, the swirls coming off the zombie will now turn red.

HOW TO...
DISCOVER FOSSILS

Fossils are some of the toughest things to find in Minecraft - here's how you give yourself the best shot!

WHERE TO FIND FOSSILS

Fossils can only be found underground in the Overworld, and only in two biomes: Deserts and Swampland, including their variants. They're most common at around 15-20 blocks below sea level, and if you're checking the game co-ordinates you'd want the Y value to be between 40 and 49. Despite this, they're still exceptionally rare, so don't be surprised if it takes a long time to find any! From the Caves & Cliffs update (version 1.17) onwards, it's possible for fossils to spawn anywhere from levels -63 to 320 of the map.

STRUCTURE

Fossils are mostly made of bone blocks, which can be crafted into (or from) bone meal. They should be mined with a pickaxe, and when placed under a note block they make a unique xylophone sound. Parts of the fossil structures are often replaced with coal ore (or, at very low depths, diamond ore).

TIP: There are eight types of fossil in total – four skulls and four spines.

NETHER FOSSILS

Perhaps the easiest – though hardly safest – way to find fossils is in the Soul Sand Valley biome of the Nether, which is strewn with half-formed fossil skeletons of long-departed Nether beasts. These Nether fossils are slightly different to the Overworld type because they're only made of bone. There are 14 variants in total, although they all look fairly similar!

TIP: You can also find bone blocks in some Bastion Remnant loot chests.

FOSSIL HUNTING TECHNIQUES

Unfortunately, there are no shortcuts to finding fossils. The quickest thing to do is explore – they can intersect with caves, so it's a lot easier to find them in existing tunnels rather than digging new ones. Of course, the problem here is that caves can and do divert themselves from where fossils generate by crossing into another biome, so don't stray too far. Don't forget to light dark areas, as they might hide an exposed block you can't see in the dark. Also look out for underground ravines, as fossils can be exposed inside them.

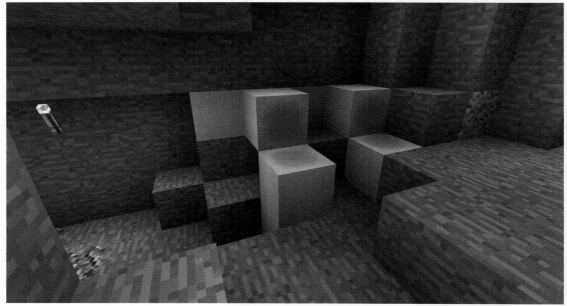

HOW TO...
HIDE YOUR
BASE

Want to make a secret entrance for your base? Here are some techniques...

TREE TRUNK ENTRANCE

Trees are common in all biomes, so they make great cover for a secret entrance. Not all trees are suitable, though – the best for this type of secret entrance are dark oaks, because their trunks are already quite thick and irregular so you can build one up without arousing too much suspicion! Extend the trunk out a little, carve out the interior, then put in a dark oak door so it blends in with the wood. You can camouflage the door with grass, ferns, leaf blocks and more wooden logs to create a near-invisible entrance that's hard to stumble across until you're right next to it.

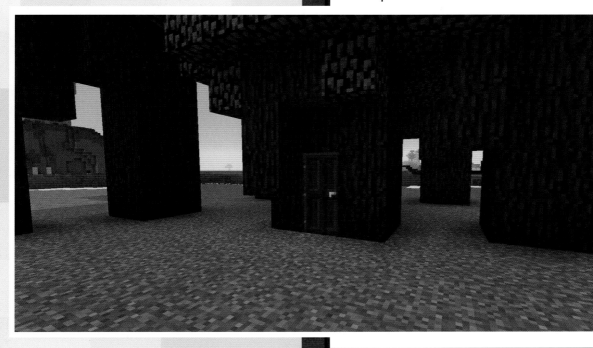

UNDERWATER
ENTRANCE

and off without actually extinguishing the flames or making it obvious to others where the mechanism is hidden!

UNDERWATER ENTRANCE

The secret to building a well-hidden underwater entrance is to make sure it can't be seen from above – build an overhang, then cover it with sand to stop it being easy to spot. You'll also need to make sure the entrance isn't TOO well lit from inside to prevent light leakage giving you away. Keeping water out is harder, but you can wall it up or dig a small trench inside. Remember that if you're building underwater, you need to make sure it's possible to get to the surface easily without drowning!

SECRET DOOR (PISTONS

TIP: Use sea pickles and glow lichen to disguise where the light comes from underwater.

SECRET DOOR (PISTONS)

Secret doors are quite hard to build, but a lever activating a pair of sticky pistons can make it possible. The trick with this kind of secret doorway is to make sure it blends as seamlessly into the walls as possible. If you make it obvious that something's out of place, it will be clear to visitors that there's a doorway being hidden. You definitely don't want the pistons to be visible! Obscure the switch in a fireplace so you can turn it on

SECRET DOOR (PAINTING)

A much simpler secret door can be made with a painting. First, carve out the doorway as you normally would, then put two blank signs in the gap, one on top of the other. Now place a painting in the block on the bottom left of the doorway so it covers the signs. And that's it! Now you can jump in and out of the painting

SECRET
DOOR

at your own will. Be careful not to punch the painting, otherwise it will pop off the wall, and make sure no one sees what you're doing. This isn't very secure and anyone can easily follow you!

TIP: If you make a secret door behind a painting, place it one block up from the floor so you have to jump in and out to disguise it further!

HOW TO...
SURVIVE ANYWHERE

Minecraft has tonnes of biomes to survive in, so how do you endure its hardest challenges?

MOUNTAINS

The main threat in Mountains is that you'll slip and fall, so remember to sneak near ledges. Wear leather armour to protect yourself if you manage to stumble into some powder snow, and watch out for charging goats! Food is very scarce at any height in this biome, so make sure you bring something to eat.

DESERTS

In Deserts, the best way to survive is to rely on villages and desert temples. Food is virtually impossible to find, and it's difficult to hide from mobs. Husks in particular can quickly swarm against you if you're not quick and inflict the Hunger effect, so steer clear of them! Wood is quite rare, but you can harvest sticks from dead bushes.

OCEAN

Being stuck in the ocean is no joke! If you don't have a boat, you'll probably be in serious trouble. Stay away from monuments, which are swarming with guardians, and try not to crash into dolphins. If you have a small amount of land to use, you can dry kelp in a furnace or fish for food!

UNDERGROUND

There's almost no food or wood underground, so bring as much as you can carry – but if you need to stay down there, you can farm crops with enough light and dirt. Abandoned mines should have some food and plenty of wood, but ideally you don't want to be underground for too long as the danger is great.

JUNGLE

Dense with leaf blocks, the shade in Jungles can also shelter mobs during the day, so take care! Luckily, it's easy to get food from melons and wood from the trees – just be aware that traversing the terrain will be slow. Use vines to climb up high, and you'll be able to move more quickly, and if you find water, stick to that for clear passage.

TIP: Carry wheat to craft cocoa beans into cookies in Jungles.

SWAMPS

Slimes and witches are common in swamps, and while it's usually quite easy to cross them, some might slow you down with their shallow-yet-inconvenient water. It's hard to fight witches when you're bogged down – try climbing up tree vines so they can't get you with their potions! Mushrooms also provide an extra food source in Swampland biomes – just remember to craft a bowl!

TIP: Carry a fishing rod to get food from any body of water.

HOW TO... BREED VILLAGERS

> Want more villagers? You can encourage them to breed!

BREEDING

Unlike other breedable mobs in the game, villagers can't be forced to breed by the player. However, you CAN create the conditions required for villagers to breed. As with any mob, if two villagers are in breeding mode close by, they'll meet up and spawn a child. While putting most mobs into breeding mode is as simple as feeding them the right food, villagers need a much more flexible set of conditions to be met!

WILLINGNESS

The first condition is willingness. To make two villagers willing to breed, you first have to raise their level from the default. One way to do this is by feeding them – you can throw three bread loaves, 12 carrots, 12 potatoes or 12 beetroot at a villager and let them hold it in their inventory to make them willing. You can also trade with them to increase willingness, or allow farmer villagers to harvest food and distribute it to them! If their willingness gets high enough, they'll enter the next phase of the process…

TIP: If farmers have access to crops, they can and will feed other villagers automatically.

POPULATION

As well as being willing to breed, the village population must be low enough. A village is any area with three beds that have two blocks of space above them, where those beds can also be reached by a villager. To breed, there must be more beds than there are villagers. If the villager is willing to breed AND the population is less than one villager per valid bed, a child villager will be spawned. Twenty minutes after that, they'll grow into an adult villager.

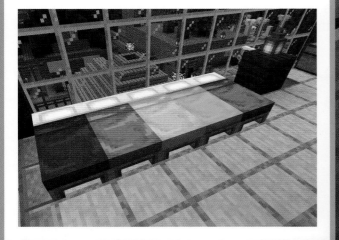

AFTERWARDS

Once a villager has bred, they can learn a trade by assigning themselves to an unassigned job block (e.g. a cartographer on a cartography table), allowing you to trade with them. If you increase the number of villagers in a village to 10, they'll try to spawn an iron golem to protect the village (assuming no golem has been detected elsewhere). You can also use breeding to create new villages – though take care if you do this close to your base, as villages attract raids and zombie sieges!

TIP: Attacking villagers angers them AND reduces their willingness to breed.

HOW TO... FARM HONEY

Honey can cure you, feed you AND be turned into a unique sticky block. How do you get it?

CRAFT A HIVE

First, you need to find some bees. They spawn in natural bee nests, which spawn in temperate forests on oak or birch trees. You need to harvest three honeycomb for the crafting recipe, so start by planting flowers near the bees and letting them collect pollen. When they take it back to the nest, the hive will fill with honey until it's dripping from the entrance. Light a campfire under the nest (to stop the bees getting angry) and use shears on it to collect three honeycomb. You can now craft them with six wood planks to make a hive.

FILLING A HIVE

Once you've placed the hive where you want, you need to encourage bees to enter it. Holding flowers will cause bees to follow you, so find some bees and lure them from the nest to your hive. You can use the flowers on them to cause them to breed, and the babies will enter the nearest hive or nest.

TIP: Bees attempt to return to the nearest hive at night or when it rains.

FARMING HONEY

Bees make honey by visiting flowers and bringing the pollen back to their nest or hive. Planting a variety of flowers close to the hive will mean they make honey quicker. You may wish to build an enclosure around them so they can't wander too far from the hive, and naturally you can build multiple hives in one place. You can extract the honey by placing a campfire underneath the hive and using an empty glass bottle on it. Take care – a campfire can burn bees that land on it, so remember to extinguish it when the honey is collected.

HONEY & HONEYCOMB

Like drinking milk, eating honey will remove any status effects (such as Poison!) you have. Unlike milk, it also restores six hunger points. Four honey bottles can be crafted into a sticky honey block, which slows down mobs that walk on it. Four honeycombs can be crafted into honeycomb blocks, which are mostly decorative but make a flute sound if placed under a note block.

TIP: In the Java Edition, you can place carpet tiles on top of a campfire to stop bees getting too close.

21 END TIPS

The End is the last place you'll visit in Minecraft - here's how to master it

1 Some blocks behave differently in the End. Crops will never grow, for example, and Nether portals won't activate.

2 You can build in the End, but leave the entry platform free, otherwise your build will be deleted when you enter.

3 Shulkers are the only aggressive mob in the game not to drop experience when you kill them.

4 You can collect items stored in an ender chest from any other ender chest in the game – and other players can't see them.

5 You can use snowballs to destroy End crystals while fighting the ender dragon.

6 If you connect a dragon head to a power source, it will open and close its mouth.

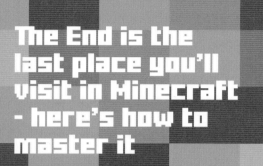

6 DRAGON HEADS

7 Shulker boxes can be dyed all 16 colours, which is useful for telling them apart when used as storage!

8 Ender chests can't be mined without a Silk Touch pickaxe. If broken normally, they'll just drop obsidian and you'll have to re-craft the chest to get at the items inside!

9 End ships, which float near some End cities, contain two rare things: the dragon head block and the elytra.

10 End ships are also one of the few places you can find enchanted diamond gear!

8
USING AN
ENDER CHEST

12
SHULKER
ATTACKS

21
GETTING
BACK IS
TOUGH!

11 The very centre of the End, where the dragon spawns, is surrounded by a large void, which you can cross using an End gateway once the dragon is dead.

12 Shulkers attack with an anti-gravity blast – if you get hit, try to make sure you don't fall to your death!

13 The End is very hard to get around – throw ender pearls to move between floating islands, and don't fall into the void!

14 There's no way to respawn in the End when you die – even a respawn anchor won't work here!

15 Compasses and clocks don't work in the End, but lodestones and maps do!

16 The large purple chorus plants drop chorus fruit, which can be eaten to replenish hunger – but which will also teleport you a few blocks in a random direction!

17 Cooking chorus fruit will turn it into popped chorus fruit, which you can use to craft purpur blocks.

18 End rods are the only light source in the End, and can be placed horizontally or vertically on any surface.

19 Make sure you take lots of food and wood with you to the End, as there's not much of either around!

20 End stone is the only block type on which you can plant chorus flowers, which grow into chorus trees (in any dimension).

21 Getting back to the centre of the End to leave is really difficult, so make sure you leave yourself some pointers!

BONUS SURVIVAL SEEDS

If you want to play on some interesting worlds, we've got some great survival seeds for whatever version you're playing!

JAVA EDITION

Tested on version 1.16.x

Huge Mushroom Plains Island: 805874225920322420
Double Villages: 805874225920322420
Ice Spikes: 1372204
Frozen Ocean Mushroom Island: -6314606324369970897

Frozen Ruins: -2697441784600137019
Desert Tower Village: 02091982
Acacia Island: -573947210
Sea Port Village With Ruins: -1782416884
Shipwreck Island: 0129764312587
Badlands Biome: 15913680

ACACIA ISLAND

BEDROCK EDITION

Tested on version 1.16.x

Forest Island: 1512233509
Zombie Village and Ruined Portal: 517249234
Ice Spikes and Pillager Outpost: 2223210

Mushroom Island Sea: -1675222121
Zombie Village: 1228769862
Survival Island Archipelago: 22002205
Desert City: 5644877779
Monument Survival Island: 5562118
Beached Shipwreck: -244885508
Huge Badlands: 39372

DESERT CITY